Trump Trial: Stormy

Stormy Daniels Testifies Against Trump

by Matthew Russell Lee
Inner City Press
May 6-10, 2024

TABLE OF CONTENTS

Chapter 1: Jail for Contempt?

Chapter 2: Trump II

Chapter 3: Evangelical

Chapter 4: The Horseman

Chapter 5: Trump Trial Day May 6, 2024

Chapter 6: Stormy Daniels Dishes on Lake Tahoe, Parking Lot Threats

Chapter 7: Prophet in Collect Pond Park

Chapter 8: Stormy

Chapter 9: May 7, 2024 Trump Trial Day May 7, 2024

Chapter 10: Chapter 10: Stormy Daniels Disclaims Name of Strip Dancing Tour as Is Shown Nasty Tweets

Chapter 11: Court Artist

Chapter 12: Stormy II, Pearl Necklace

Chapter 13: May 9, 2024 Trump Trial Day

Chapter 14: Madeleine Westerhout

Chapter 15: May 10, 2024 Trump Trial Day

Chapter 16: Jeff McConney

Chapter 17: Deb Terasoff

Chapter 1: Jail for Contempt?

On Monday, May 6 the Trump trial began with Justice Merchan threatening to jail Trump for violations of his gag order.

He said 10 violations were enough and that among his job is protecting the dignity of the court.

Then the first witness was called: Jeff McConney, now retired Trump Organization controller.

Trump's lawyer Emil Bove objected without being sustained to the entry into evidence of several financial records, and a Government Ethics Office form.

Trump filed a disclosure that he paid a reimbursement to Michael Cohen in 2017.

By lunch, Bove would emphasize that Trump make the disclose, that McConney rarely spoke with Trump, and that the accounting software used in the Trump Organization was antiquated and so, by implication, legal expenses could mean many different things.

Would Justice Merchan actually order Trump jailed? How would it work - Rikers? And might it, in fact, help Trump's campaign? Would it suspend the trial?

Chapter 2: Trump II

I've had a lot of lawsuits
The people who bought condos
For only my name
(which I took off)
Or me suing reporters
Before the anti-SLAPP laws

But sitting in the f*cking cold courtroom
Watch Bragg's minions
Showing Merchan my tweets
It's slowly driving me crazy
Maybe I do need an editor
On Truth Social
Maybe I've lost the magic
Maybe not

Chapter 3: Evangelical

God and guns they say we care about
But there's also abortion
And Holy Land defense.
Trump didn't seem the most natural fit

But after he torched Ted and Marco
Where else was there to go?

He did what he said he would on Roe
And wouldn't have talked with Hamas
Whatever the Art of the Deal

Like Cyrus of Persia some say
Without the pallets of cash
And the centrifuge

What we read from New York
That blogger in the back?
We'll see how we feel
When November 5 comes.

Chapter 4: The Horseman

The horseman was at the court
With a crowd to welcome Trump
One had an enormous flag
A jewel-spangled banner cap

Readers said he was sh*t
Like came out the back of the horse.
On January 6 he had been there
Lost his job after 20 days in jail

"Insurrectionists" attract
Trump waved through the window

Chapter 5 - May 6, 2024 Trump Trial Day

Trump has arrived - blue suit, red tie - and is whispering with his lawyer Todd Blanche to his left. Emil Bove is to his right in the lead counsel / cross-examiner's seat.
All rise!
Clerk: This is People of the State of NY versus Donald J. Trump!

Justice Merchan: Before the court is the People's motion for contempt. Mr. Trump, in a moment I will hand down my ruling finding you in criminal contempt for the tenth time. Going forward, the Court will have a consider jail.

Justice Merchan: I am concerned about the ramifications of putting you in jail. But I have a job to do, to compel respect for the dignity of the court. Your behavior constitutes a direct attack on the rule. If I need to, I will.

Clerk: Case on trial continues.

Justice Merchan: A fresh witness today.

Prosecutor: The People will be calling Jeffrey McConney [Trump Organization Controller and SVP]

Trump's lawyer Emil Bove: We'd like to address objections outside the presence of the jury

Justice Merchan: Are you asking to dismiss the jury?

Trump's lawyer Bove: I don't think it will take that long.

Justice Merchan: I'll have you do that at the sidebar.

Bove: I only found out about the witness yesterday.

Justice Merchan: We'll have them one by one.

Trump's lawyer Blanche: The witness after this one, we have an objection to them testifying at all.

Justice Merchan: I'll hear you then. Get the jury.

[Jury entering!]

[Here's from today's contempt order by Justice Merchan: "Defendant is hereby put on notice that if appropriate and warranted, future violations of its lawful orders will be punishable by incarceration.

Prosecutor: Mr. McConney, please describe your education
McConney: Baruch College; hired by the Trump Organization in 1987. Now I'm retired.
Prosecutor: Did you sign a separation agreement?
McConney: Yes. The payments are now complete. I did tax prep for 50 years

Prosecutor: Are you here under subpoena?
McConney: Yes.
Prosecutor: Who is paying for your lawyer?
McConney: The Trump Organization.
Prosecutor: Who ran it?
McConney: President Trump. He was the brains behind it. He was my boss.

Prosecutor: Have you spoke with him since your retired last February?
McConney. Uh, no.

Prosecutor: How are Trump Organization entities owned?
McConney: Each one is separately owned. Ultimately, the Trust.
Prosecutor: Have you reviewed People's 86?
McConney: Yes

Prosecutor: What does it say at the top?
McConney: The Donald J. Trump Revocable Trust.
Prosecutor: Who were on it?
McConney: President Trump, Donald Trump, Jr. and Allen Weisselberg.
Prosecutor: Did you oversee the general ledger?
McConney: Yes

Prosecutor: Did you supervise Deb Tarasoff?
McConney: Yes.
Prosecutor: Did the Trump Tower accounting team cover all entities?
McConney: All except gold course and hotels.
Prosecutor: Who enters information into the general ledger?
McConney: The accounting staff.

Prosecutor: Does the team also cover Mr. Trump's personal accounts?
McConney: Yes. They're coded DJT.
Prosecutor: In 2017 did Mr. Trump use a Capital One account as his main account?
McConney: Yes.
[Note: Capital One now applying for Federal OKs to buy Discover

Prosecutor: Did you interact with Mr. Trump about the reports?
McConney: I'd hand-deliver the reports. One time President Trump told me, You're fired. When he got off the phone he said, You're not fired, but pay attention to my bills, don't just pay them

Prosecutor: Did the Trump Organization ever cut a check if no invoice was submitted?
McConney: Never.
Prosecutor: Who has authority to approve invoices?
McConney: President Trump, Eric Trump, Don Jr., Ivanka when she was working with us, a few others

Prosecutor: One many signatures were required on checks?

McConney: Below $10,000 only one signature. Over $10,000, two signatures.

Prosecutor: If a lawyer receives payment, is it taxable?

McConney? If an outside attorney, I assume so. [Sips from water bottle]

Prosecutor: Did you review the files on this thumb drive earlier today?

McConney: Much earlier today, yes.

Prosecutor: Have you emailed with Michael Cohen?

McConney: Yes.

Prosecutor: We ask to admit these exhibits.

Trump's lawyer Bove: We object to several

Prosecutor: Are you familiar with Michael Cohen?

McConney: We both worked there. I spoke with him by the coffee machine.

Prosecutor: What was his position?

McConney: He said he was a lawyer.

Prosecutor: Did he ask to be reimbursed?

McConney: Sometime in Jan 2017

McConney: He was supposed to leave January 20, 2017 but it got moved to January 27. He had some complaint about his last year's bonus.

Prosecutor: Show People's Exhibit 35 to the witness, court & parties only. What is it?

McConney: The bank statement Allen gave me

Prosecutor: Did you keep it in the files?

McConney: Yes. In a book in a locked drawer in my office.

Prosecutor: People's 36. Did you take these notes while Mr. Weisselberg spoke to you?

McConney: Yes. They were stapled to the bank statement.

Prosecutor: What is this bank statement:

McConney: It's Essential Consultants, First Republic Bank account. $130,035. To Keith M. Davidson Associates, PLC. $130,000. That's Allen Weisselberg's handwriting, Grossed out, then divided by 12

Prosecutor: Why $180,000?

McConney: The $130,000 to Michael Cohen, $50,000 to Red Finch.

Prosecutor: What's the grossing up?
McConney: To cover taxes. Between Federal, NYS and NYC taxes.
Prosecutor: Where is Mr. Cohen live?
McConney: You want the address? No? NYC

Prosecutor: So 35,000 a month?
McConnell: Yes. We'd wire it each month starting Feb 1, 2017.
Prosecutor: Did you take notes? People's 36.
McConnel; Those are my notes. Bonus $50,000, then $180,000, grossing up the 180, so it's $420,000, wire from DJT

Prosecutor: With the grossing up, was this an expensive reimbursement like others?
McConnell: No.
Prosecutor: Let me show you this exhibit --
Trump's lawyer Bove: Objection!
Judge Merchan: Please approach
[Whispered sidebar ensues]

Justice Merchan: Objection
Prosecutor: Please read this
McConney: I asked for an invoice. A lot of people ask for money- we need an invoice.

Michael wrote, Remind me of the monthly amount. I replied, $35,000. Then he wrote, "Pursuant to the retainer agreement"

McConney: Then Allen wrote to me, OK to pay per agreement with Don and Eric.
Prosecutor: Who was Don?
McConney: Don Jr.
Prosecutor: Did you forward to legal department?
McConney: No.
Prosecutor: Would a legal retainer payment usually be sent there?
McConney: Yes

Prosecutor: You posted this to legal expenses?
McConney: I did. The code was 51505.
Prosecutor: Did the Trump Organization's outside accounts have access to this?
McConney: Not directly, but through the reports.
Prosecutor: Did Mr. Cohen invoice each month?
A: Yes

Prosecutor: What did you do in this time frame for checks?

McConney: We'd have to get them down to DC for signature. It was brand new for us. I wrote, "DJT needs to sign check."

Prosecutor: I offer 37c

Trump's lawyer Bove: Objection

Justice Merchan: Overruled

Prosecutor: More 37 series exhibits.

Justice Merchan: Objection noted and overruled.

Prosecutor: What's this?

McConney: Emails with Michael Cohen, Deb and Allen and me - invoices, here from May. Then, I told Deb to put a stop on Check 2639, we couldn't find it

Prosecutor: Please read this one.

McConney: Invoice in July, Michael wrote to Allen, hope you are enjoying the summer despite the nonsense, and the invoice.

Prosecutor: And this one?

McConney: August. From 30 Rockefeller Plaza. And here, September.

McConney: In this one Michael wrote that he hoped Allen's Florida home wasn't damaged by hurricane - and the invoice.
Prosecutor: When Allen forwarded it to you without any additional message, do you take it to mean, Pay it?
McConney: Yes

Prosecutor: Did the payments stop in December?
McConney: Yes.
Justice Merchan: Let's take a break.

They've back
Prosecutor: What is this print out?
McConney: Which company paid which invoice. This has DJT, his personal accounts. And checks to Michael Cohen up to January 5, 2018. Total for 2017, $440,000
Trump's lawyer Bove: Objection
Justice Merchan: Overruled

Prosecutor: And in this wider data base of legal expenses, were they any others involving Michael Cohen?

McConney: No.
Prosecutor: What's this?
McConney: The detailed general ledger
Prosecutor: Does it say legal retainer?
McConney: Yes.

Prosecutor: Are you aware of IRS Form 1099s?
McConney: We generate them, send a copy to recipient, and a copy to IRS.
Prosecutor: What's this?
McConney: A 1099-MISC for 2017 from DJT Revocable Trust to Michael D. Cohen, Esq. Box 7 says, Non-employee compensation

Prosecutor: Are you aware of the Office of Government Ethics or OGE?
McConney: Yes.
Prosecutor: Did you file for Mr. Trump?
McConney: Yes, Form 278-E, a conflict-of-interest form. He filed in 2015 to 2020, since then I don't know, he's a candidate.

Prosecutor: I offer these into evidence.
Trump's lawyer Bove: Objection!
Justice Merchan: Please approach.

[sidebar]
Justice Merchan: Overruled.
Prosecutor: Please publish the form for the jury. What does this say:
McConney: Mr. Cohen sought reimbursement

Prosecution: What range was this?
McConnell: This was between $100,000 and $250,000.
Prosecution: What that consistent with the $180,000 you discussed with Allen Weisselberg?
McConney: Yes.
Prosecutor: No further question.
Justice Merchan: Cross-examination?

Trump's lawyer Emil Bove: You rarely spoke to President Trump, did you?
McConney: I did not.
Bove: He never asked you to make these entries?
McConney: He did not.
Bove: And Mr. Weisselberg didn't tell you President Trump told him to do it?
McConney: No.

Trump's lawyer Bove: Here is Michael Cohen's signature block - does it say "fixer"?
McConney: It does not.
Bove: Michael Cohen was basically a vendor to President Trump, right?
McConney. Yes.
Bove: He said he had an outside firm?
McConney: Yes.

Trump's lawyer Bove: You don't know if Michael Cohen did legal work for President Trump with regard to Summer Zervos?
McConney: I don't.
Bove: Things were in flux - President Trump's office was in DC, not NYC?
McConney: I don't remember seeing him in NY at all

Trump's lawyer Bove: I'd like to show Defense Exhibit H 10
Prosecutor: Objection! May we approach?
Justice Merchan: Sure.
[Sidebar]
Justice Merchan: Objection sustained.
Bove: There were two trustees, one of President Trump's sons and Allen

Weisselberg?
A: Yes

Trump's lawyer Bove: You understand that negative news would hurt the business?
McConney: I'm not a marketing guy.
Bove: But the Trump Organization hired marketing people, right?
McConney: Yes.
Bove: The MDS system was antiquated, right? Old categories?
A: Yes.

Trump's lawyer Bove: Let's talk about your handwritten notes, "X2 for taxes."
McConney: Allen was rattling off things that I had to write down.
Bove: But he was not a tax accountant, right?
McConney: He was not.

Trump's lawyer Bove: This First Republic document - you just filed it?
McConney: Yes
Bove: You don't know anything about Red Finch, do you?
McConney: I do not.
Bove: Retainer agreements can be verbal,

can't they?
McConney: They can.

Trump's lawyer Bove: The 1st 3 payment were paid out of the Trump, and the remainder from President Trump's personal account?
McConney: Yes.
Bove: This 1099 doesn't have any space to distinguish legal fees versus expenses incurred, right?
McConney: It does not.

Trump's lawyer Bove: This Office of Government Affairs form, the payment to Michael Cohen were disclosed, right?
McConney: Yes.
Bove: Nothing further.
Justice Merchan: Redirect?
Prosecutor: Do expense reimbursements usually get disclosed to the IRS?
McConney: No

Prosecutor: Have you come to know that there were things Mr. Weisselberg kept you in the dark about?
Trump's lawyer Bove: Objection!

Justice Merchan: Overruled.
McConney: Yes.
Re-cross:
Bove: It was all disclosed to the IRS?
McConney: Yes.

Justice Mercan: We'll break.

They've back.
Trump's lawyer Blanche: Half an hour ago, we learned who the next witness is - and we have some objections. Invoices from Michael Cohen are not business records of the Trump Organization. If she stamped them, sure

Justice Merchan: I'm going to allow them in as res gestae: part of the crime.
Trump's lawyer Blanche: On People's 42, Capital One records, we believe this witness a Trump Organization employee
Prosecutor: It's Deb Tarasoff. They are canceled checks

Justice Merchan: I will allow them in. Bring on the witness.
Prosecutor: Ms. Tarasoff, are you employed?

Tarasoff: Yes, with the Trump Organization. It's a real estate company.
Prosecutor: Who is the owner?
Tarasoff: Correct me if I'm wrong, Mr. Trump.

Prosecutor: Your education?
Tarasoff: High school. Then I worked at Liberty Mutual, then for a lawyer who dealt with real estate, parking lots. I cared for my girls. Finally, Trump Organization.
Prosecutor: How many entities in the Trump Organization?
A: A bunch.

Prosecutor: What was Mr. Weisselberg's management style?
Tarasoff: He had his hands in everything.
Prosecutor: Did he interact often with Mr. Trump?
Tarasoff: Yes.
Prosecutor: What system did you use?
Tarasoff: MDS. I would see invoices, cut a check, mail it

Prosecutor: Up to what amount could Allen Weisselberg approve?

Tarasoff: $10,000. Above that, you'd need Don Jr., Eric or Mr. Trump.
Prosecutor: How would you get DJT checks signed?
Tarasoff: I'd take them to Rhona, she'd take them in for Mr. Trump to sign them.

Prosecutor: Would he ever refuse to sign a check?
Tarasoff: He would write Void on it.
Prosecutor: How would you know it was him?
Tarasoff: He would use a Sharpie, I'd recognize it.
Prosecutor: I'm handing you a thumb drive.
Trump's lawyer Blanche: We object

Justice Merchan: They are admitted.
Prosecutor: How did you get the checks down to Mr. Trump in DC ?
Tarasoff: FedEx.
Prosecutor: People's 37A. Blow up the top e-mail. Did you receive it?
Tarasoff: Yes. Feb 14, 2017. I was told to pay & post to legal expenses

Prosecutor: This $70,000 check, 138, who signed it?
Tarasoff: Eric and Allen Weisselberg.
Prosecutor: And this email?
Tarasoff: Jeff McConney said to pay it. There is my stamp.
Prosecutor: And this check, did you put a stop payment order?
Tarasoff: Yes.

After a break, they've back.
Prosecutor: While we were talking through those exhibits, I think I missed one. What is this?
Tarasoff: It's another invoice, June 2017.
Prosecutor: And how much is the check for?
Tarasoff: $35,000.

Prosecutor: I have nothing further.
Justice Merchan: Your witness.
Trump's lawyer Blanche: Would you describe the Trump Organization as a family business?
Tarasoff: Yes.
Blanche: Was President Trump around less while he was running for President?
Tarasoff: Yes.

Trump's lawyer Blanche: The checks that we just went through for the last hour and a half (chuckles), they are all signed, except the one that got lost?
Tarasoff: Yes
Blanche: You weren't present for President Trump's talks with Mr. Weisselberg?
A: I was not

Trump's lawyer Blanche: No more questions.
Justice Merchan: Mr. Tarasoff, you may step down. Counsel, please approach.
[During sidebar, Trump speaks with his other lawyer Susan Necheles, who slides over. Then"]
Justice Merchan: Jurors, we will break early

[Jurors leave]
Prosecutor: We'd likc to recall a witness to go over some tweets and Truths... We called Ms. Longstreet on Friday before Hope Hicks - but she has more.... It's just not true that counsel has not had notice of our exhibits.

Trump's lawyer Blanche: I'm looking at the Jan 2024 witness list, Ms. Longstreet's not on it. They should have told us she had reviewed

more posts.
Justice Merchan: When will you call her?
Prosecutor: We have another witness tomorrow. So, Thursday or Friday.

Justice Merchan: How much longer, People?
Prosecutor: Roughly, two weeks from tomorrow.
Justice Merchan: See you tomorrow.

Chapter 6: At Trump Trial Stormy Daniels Dishes on Lake Tahoe and Parking Lot Threats

Tuesday, May 7 at the Trump trial, the Stormy day it would be, began with a witness from Random House, reading quotes from two of Trump's books to show that he was and is a micro-manager.

Then Stormy took the stand.

She spoke quickly, sometimes too quickly for the court reporter, Justice Merchan said. She met Trump at a celebrity golf tournament in 2006 in Lake Tahoe and, after a two hours conversation in his suite, returned from the bathroom only to find him posing in boxers on the bed.

The prosecutor had said some details would be necessary, but when Stormy said missionary Justice Merchan sustained an objection. So too on looking up at the ceiling. Stormy invited Trump to see her at a strip club in New York - because it was a public space she said.

There was a threat in a Las Vegas parking lot, which Stormy said led her to want to get her story out. Then she decided that selling story to Trump and Michael Cohen would be just as good. The morning ended with names of others who heard the story on the screen.

Susan Necheles was on desk for the cross-examination. Strategically, better than a man going it. But would she come off too judgmental? This was an aspect of voir dire jury selection not focused on enough (but in

Inner City Press' book on the Trump Trial Voir Dire / Jury Selection

Chapter 7: Prophet in Collect Pond Park

The end must be near
With all these police
Whole neighborhoods shut down
For the trial of a single man

I walk with my cross
And shepherd's bell
And no one hears me
It's as if I am a ghost
Or it has already ended

[Some say jacket says Lincoln, JFK and Trump]

Chapter 8: Stormy

When I went to the Harrah's penthouse
The orange man was there in pajamas
I told him he looked like Hugh Hefner
Then asked for a chance on The Apprentice

After I looked in his Dopp kit
He struck a pose in his boxers
Soon I was under him
And now I'm here in court.

Sure it's helped my career
This single short act with a tall man
Still I can say I hate the orange turd
Why'd he have to sue me for fees?

Now this old crow
Glowering at me
And it's not over
This cross I'm on

Chapter 9: May 7, 2024 Trump Trial Day

Trump has arrived, blue suit and yellow tie. This time his lawyer Susan Necheles sets up in the lead counsel seat to his right. Apparently, she'd be doing the Stormy cross examination today. But - contempt motion or argument first?

All rise!
Clerk: This is the People of the State of New

York versus Donald J. Trump!

Justice Merchan: Anything we need to discuss?

Trump's lawyer Necheles: We are informed that Stormy Daniels is the second witness today, we oppose any details of sexual acts

Justice Mercan: Other than just, We had sex?

Prosecutor: Your Honor only limited details as to Karen McDougal, not Stormy Daniels. The details are important, the sex act - only certain details are unnecessary

Prosecutor Susan Hoffinger: We'll get into the conversation they had in the hotel and how the sexual act came about, how she felt about it. We will not get into genitalia.

Trump's lawyer Necheles: There is no need for this. This is a case about books and records.

Justice Merchan: This woman has credibility issues, so details are important. I will allow them. Call your witness... Oh, the jury. Bring the jury in first

[Jury entering!]

Prosecutor: The People call Susan Franklin...
[Witness is sworn and seated]
Prosecutor: Where do you work?
Franklin: Penguin Random House and its imprints. I am here under subpoena.
Prosecutor: Are you familiar with "Trump: How to Get Rich"?
Franklin: Yes.

Prosecutor: For that book and another have you reviewed the excerpts, People's 413 and 414, Trump: Think Like a Billionaire?
Franklin: Yes.
Prosecutor: What does is say under the title?
Franklin: "Big deals from the star of The Apprentice"

Prosecutor: What's the largest word on the cover?
Franklin: Trump.
Prosecutor: What percentage of the cover does it take up?
Franklin: Thirty percent.
Prosecutor: And on Trump: Think like a Billionaire?
Franklin: Maybe 25%.

Prosecutor: People's 413A.
Franklin: Be like a general.
Prosecutor: This?
Franklin: If you don't know all the details, you're setting yourself up
Prosecutor: 413C?
Franklin: "Sometimes you still have to screw them... Like it says in the Bible, An eye for an eye"

Prosecutor: And this?
Franklin: "All the women on The Apprentice flirts with me. That's to be expected...
Prosecutor: 414, page 41
Franklin: "With a decorator, make sure to see all of the invoices. You should be double checking."

Prosecutor: And this?
Franklin: I always sign my checks, to make sure where my money is going. Check through your bills. My parents hammered frugality into me at an early age.
Prosecutor: People's 414-c.
Franklin: Watch the bottom line. Weisselberg is tough

Prosecutor: Lastly, 414-d

Franklin: Always look at the numbers yourself. In the 1980s Jeff McConney prepared my small shot. I told him, "You're fired." I meant, question every payment. Jeff got the message, now does a terrific job.

Prosecutor: No further questions

Trump's lawyer Todd Blanche: Do you know how much the ghostwriter did?

Franklin: I don't.

Blanche: Who designs the cover?

Franklin: We have a department.

Blanche: So it is not entirely the author?

Franklin: We want to make the author happy.

Blanche: Nothing more

Justice Merchan: Re-direct?

Prosecutor: Let's turn to 413 f - h, wc offer them.

Trump's lawyer Blanche: May we approach, your Honor?

[Whispered sidebar ensues - during which, Susan Necheles remains at defense table, talking with Trump]

[Back from sidebar]
Prosecutor: We enter these into evidence.
Justice Merchan: Yes. Objection overruled.
Prosecutor: What's this?
Franklin: The epigraph page. The largest quote is by "DJT."
Prosecutor: 413h
Franklin: Meredith was just outside my office door

Prosecutor: And this?
Franklin: Thanks offered to Random House staff.
Prosecutor: Does this indicate an author very involved in the book?
Franklin: Yes.
Prosecutor: This?
Franklin: God is in the details. Sign your own checks. People see it and they screw you less

Prosecutor: No further questions.
Re-cross.
Trump's lawyer Blanche: Leave 414g up. We don't have the exhibit, so if we could ask the People... Blow up the last page. What does it say?

Franklin: Meredith McIver thanking people
Blanche: Nothing more

Justice Merchan: Counsel, please approach. [Long sidebar, during which Trump and Emil Bove talk at defense table. Then:]
Prosecutor: The People call Stormy Daniels. Please tell me about your family.
Daniels: I was born in Baton Rouge, Louisiana.

Daniels: Now I live in Florida with my partner. My parents split up when I was 4. I went to a strict Christian school, paid for by my father. I was raised by my mother.
Prosecutor: Hobbies in school?
Daniels: Newspaper editor. Four H club. Baton Rouge Ballet Co

Daniels: A friend introduced me to dancing, exotic dancing, when I was in high school. It was better than my other job, shoveling manure.
Prosecutor: Why did you move out?
Daniels: My mother was neglectful, left me alone. She wasn't even an addict

Prosecutor: Did you do nude modeling?
Daniels: Yes. You had to have credentials or credits to be the star. I went on to pose, to go on tour as a featured entertainer. I was 21.
Prosecutor: Did you work in the adult film industry?
Daniels: I was a clothed extra

Daniels: A famous adult film director saw me, and I got a contract.
Prosecutor: Do you write and direct adult films?
Daniels: There are some with dialogue, you see them on late night TV with the sex cut out. I have directed over 150 films, awards for screenplays.

Prosecutor: Have you been in films and TV?
Daniels: The 40-Year-Old Virgin... a TV show with Courtney Cox.
Prosecutor: And on a podcast?
Daniels: Yes, "Beyond the Norm." Female series killers, UFO, porn, politics.
Prosecutor: Did you discuss Mr. Trump.
A: Yes.

Prosecutor: In 2009 did you explore running for Senate in Louisiana?
Daniels: Yes (laughs) There was a "Draft Stormy" campaign, to opposed David Vitter in the Republican primary. He was anti-women, did some unsavory things. David Vitter never would debate me

Prosecutor: Let's turn to Lake Tahoe in 2006.
Daniels: I was a golf course, Wicked sponsored a hole on the golf course, yes I'm aware that it's funny.
Prosecutor: Did you meet Donald Trump?
Daniels: Yes. On the course. Wicked's owner introduced me as director

Prosecutor: What did you know about Mr. Trump?
Daniels: I hadn't seen Celebrity Apprentice. But I remember him in cameos and wrestling, it's a big deal in Louisiana.
Prosecutor: Then what?
Daniels: He asked me about my films. I saw him talk with another gentleman

Prosecutor: Do you see Mr. Trump in the courtroom? Can you identify him and an

article of clothing?
Stormy Daniels: There, with a blue suit.
Prosecutor: Take this thumb drive. People's 226, the golf room photo.
Stormy Daniels: He's in a red hat.

Prosecutor: And this photo?
Stormy Daniels: That's him on the golf course.
Prosecutor: What did you tell Mr. Trump's body guard, when he said Mr. Trump would like to take you to dinner?
Stormy Daniels: F*ck no.
Prosecutor: Did you give Keith Schiller your #?
Yes.

Prosecutor: Did you discuss the invitation with anyone?
Stormy Daniels: My media guy Mike. I was supposed to go to a Wicked dinner. I wanted to avoid it, cat fight & stuff. He told me, you should go, it'll make a great story. What could possibly go wrong? (laughs)

Stormy Daniels: I texted with Keith and arranged to go to Mr. Trump's hotel, Harrah's

Prosecutor: And next?
Daniels: Keith told me to go up to the penthouse. Keith was at the door. He said, You look nice.
Prosecutor: What were your expectations?
Daniels: Dinner

Prosecutor: What was he wearing?
Stormy Daniels: Silk pajamas. I asked him, Did you steal Hugh Hefner's pajamas? And I told me to change. He did. He came back in dress shirt and pants. This hotel room was three times the size of my apartment

Prosecutor: What did you discuss?
Stormy Daniels: I told him where I grew up, do I have siblings - I do not - did I have a boyfriend, no, at the time...
Prosecutor: Did you tell him about your hard childhood?
Daniels: Yes.
DL: Objection!
J: Sustained. "Stricken"

Stormy Daniels: So he asked about the adult film industry, whether we have unions, get residuals - usually people asking about the sexy stuff

Prosecutor: Did he ask you if you'd been tested?

Daniels: Yes. Wicked is a condom mandatory company. I'm allergic to latex

Daniels: I asked him about wrestling because he knew Vince McMahon and he'd had a cameo where he'd lost something -

Justice Merchan: Ms. Daniels, could you slow down?

Daniels: He was supposed to get his head shaved if he lost and I told him he wouldn't look good

Stormy Daniels: He said don't worry, it's all scripted.

Prosecutor: Did you ask about Melania?

Daniels: I did. He said, Don't worry, we don't even sleep in the same room. He kept cutting me off. He'd ask a question then not let me finish. I told him, You're rude

Stormy Daniels: I ended up spanking him. And after that he acted much better. He said I should be in The Apprentice. I told him, Even you don't have that much power. He said,

You remind me of my daughter, blonde & beautiful. To me it made sense.

Prosecutor: What did he say about The Apprentice?
Stormy Daniels: That he could tell me the challenge, he couldn't let me win but at least not lose right at the beginning. I wanted to direct some non-adult films, they have big budgets and better catering

Prosecutor: Did you call another friend?
Stormy Daniels: Yes, a neighbor, Alana. I had run into her and I knew she didn't believe where I was. I called her and put her on speaker. He said Hello. Why don't you come over and hang out with us. She didn't call back.

Prosecutor: At some point, did you use the restroom?
Justice Merchan: Let's take a break.

[They're back]
Prosecutor: Did you need to use the restroom?

Stormy Daniels: I was instructed by Mr. Trump to go through the bedroom to the facilities. It was a leather looking toiletry bag on the counter
Prosecutor: What was in it?
Daniels: I looked - Old Spice

Stormy Daniels: Gold tweezers. When I came out, Mr. Trump was on the bed in his boxer shorts. I was startled. I felt like the run spun in slow motion, like if you stand up too fast. I thought, Oh my God, what did I misread to get here. He was posing on the bed

Stormy Daniels: He stood up - not in a threatening manner - he said, If you ever want to get out of that trailer park
objection
Justice Merchan: Sustained. Move on.
Prosecutor: What next?
Daniels: I felt drugged
Necheles: Objection!
Justice Mercan: Overruled

[Sidebar - at defense table, Trump speaks with Bove, who again moves to far seat when Blanche returns from sidebar & whispers to

Trump]
Justice Merchan: The objection is sustained
Prosecutor: You were not drugged, right?
Stormy Daniels: There was a power imbalance

Prosecutor: Did you have sex with him on the bed?
Stormy Daniels: Missionary-
Objection
Justice Merchan: Sustained.
Daniels: I was staring at the ceiling wishing I was somewhere else
Justice Merchan: Sustained.
Prosecutor: Was he wearing a condom?
Daniels: No

Daniels: He said, That was great, we should get together again soon, honey bunch
Prosecutor: What did you say?
Daniels: Nothing. He didn't even give me his cell phone number.
Prosecutor: Did he express concern about his wife finding out?
Daniels: No

Prosecutor: Did you tell people?
Stormy Daniels: Very few. I am ashamed I hadn't stopped it. I didn't want people I was dating to find out.
Prosecutor: Did you later remember some things?
Daniels: Yes, in the book-
Objection!
Justice Merchan: Sustained. Approach

[After sidebar]
Prosecutor: Did you see him in Lake Tahoe again?
Stormy Daniels: Yes, in a night club there. Keith had called me and said Mr. Trump would be there, it would be in public. So I went.

Stormy Daniels: Ben Roethlisberger of the Steelers was there. Mr. Trump called me his little friend Stormy then said Ben would walk me to my room.
Prosecutor: Did he?
Daniels: Yes.
Prosecutor: Did you tell anyone, then?
Daniels: Another Keith, my photographer

Prosecutor: Would Mr. Trump then call you?
Stormy Daniels: Yes. I would put him on speaker, people heard him
Prosecutor: Did he know he was on speaker phone?
Daniels: No.
Prosecutor: Why did you continue to take his calls?
Daniels: My publicist bragged

Stormy Daniels: My publicist was saying, I told you so-
Justice Merchan: Please just answer the questions.
Daniels: I wanted to be on The Apprentice.
Prosecutor: Did Mr. Trump give you the number of his assistant?
Daniels: Yes. Rhona. I put her on my phone.

[Now the former Stormy Stormy contact is shown]

Prosecutor: Did you go to the launch of Mr. Trump's vodka?
Stormy Daniels: Yes. He introduced me to Karen McDougal. Then he spent most of the time talking to my friend. We lied we were

flying out of LAX on a girls' trip.
Prosecutor: Did you go to Trump Tower?
Yes

Stormy Daniels: I was dancing in a club so I invited him. It was a public place so it was safer-
objection.
Justice Merchan: Sustained.
Prosecutor: And at Trump Tower?
Daniels: He said he was still working on getting me on The Apprentice. He introduced me around

Prosecutor: Did you see Mr. Trump in LA?
Stormy Daniels: Yes, he invited me to his bungalow. By then my publicist was my boyfriend. He drove me and waited outside. That was common. Mr. Trump was watching TV, a documentary about sharks

Stormy Daniels: He kept making sexual advances. He touched my leg.
Prosecutor: How did you respond?
Daniels: I told him I was on my period. There was no progress on getting on The

Apprentice. I stopped answering his calls. But he told me Jenna Jameson would be on

Prosecutor: Did you move on? How was your life?
Stormy Daniels: Awesome. I moved to Texas, became a ranked equestrian -
Objection!
Judge Merchan: I'll allow it.
Prosecutor: Did you agree to be interviewed by In Touch?
Daniels: Yes. Someone had sold my story

Stormy Daniels: Gina [Rodriguez] told me to take control, and $15,000.
Prosecutor: How long was the interview?
Daniels: 10 or 20 minutes on the phone. They never ran the story.
Prosecutor: Did you know why?
Daniels: No.
Prosecutor: Judge, may we approach?
Yes

[After sidebar]
Prosecutor: Did you have an encounter in a parking lot in Las Vegas?
Stormy Daniels: A man approached me and

told me to not keep telling my story about Mr. Trump.
Prosecutor: Did you tell your partner?
Daniels: He was having mental issues

Prosecutor: Did you become aware your story was on The Dirty dot com.
Stormy Daniels: Yes. I don't read that site. I wanted it taken down - I'd been threatened.
Prosecutor: What did Gina say?
Daniels: She asked if she could get Keith Davidson to get it taken down?

Prosecutor: Did Keith Davidson succeed?
Stormy Daniels: Yes. It came down.
Prosecutor: In 2015 once Mr. Trump was running for President, were you told you could sell your story for more?
Daniels: Yes. I was advised by a lawyer to have a press conference

Prosecutor: Do you remember the Access Hollywood tape coming out?
Stormy Daniels: Yes. Gina told me about it. I wanted to get the story out - because of the threat.
Prosecutor: Did you find that Donald Trump

and Michael Cohen wanted to buy your story?
A: Yes.

Stormy Daniels: It would be good, my husband wouldn't find out but I'd have paperwork. I didn't care about the $130,000, the amount didn't matter to me. We no longer lived in California which is very expensive
Prosecutor: Were we presented an agreement?
A: Yes

Prosecutor: What is this?
Stormy Daniels: Keith Davidson's email to Michael Cohen. I wanted it done before the nomination.
Prosecutor: Do you mean election?
Daniels: Yes, the election. This was the side letter, I was Peggy and he was David Dennison

Prosecutor: What is this list?
Stormy Daniels: People who knew. [One is a Keith, not Davidson]
Justice Merchan: We'll break to 2.

[They've back]

Trump's lawyer Todd Blanche: We move for a mistrial based on this morning's testimony. It was prejudicial, and differs from the story she was peddling before. There was testimony about no condom, the spacing in the room, the power dynamic

Trump's lawyer Blanche: There was testimony about a second sexual advance, totally irrelevant to this case. She kept saying, it was in a public place. What is the jury to do with that? There was objection sustained but it's still prejudicial

Trump's lawyer Blanche: Guardrails didn't work. It is an issue. We're going to cross examine her shortly, presumably - but that's not really the issue. She testified today about consent, danger, it's not what she was peddling - sorry, selling - in 2016

Prosecutor: Her testimony today goes to the defendant's motive. The lack of condom has been out there for a long time. There were details she only remembered after a movie in

2019. They opened the door - they put in an exhibit saying the 2011 threat was not true

Prosecution: Some of this will come out in cross, and I hope on re-direct. She testified that she was not directly threatened, and that she did not say no.
Justice Merchan: I can rule on this. I agree there were thing that would have been better left unsaid

Justice Merchan: I do think the witness was hard to control. But I do not believe at this point a mistrial is warranted. I was surprised that there were not more objections. At one point the Court sua sponte objected.

Justice Merchan: If you want, I will give a limiting instruction as to the 2011 parking lot incident.
Trump's lawyer Susan Necheles: We have moved in advance -
Justice Merchan: That's not accurate, Ms. Necheles.
Necheles: It's why we didn't object all the time

Justice Merchan: I'm going to deny your motion for a mistrial at this time. Do you want to discuss a limiting instruction?
[Sidebar]
Justice Merchan: As discussed at the bench, we're going to take some more time - you'll be back to me by Thursday morning?
Yes.

Justice Merchan: With the consent of the defense Ms. Hoffinger has stepped out to give some instructions to her witness, to stay focused, and only answer what is asked.
[After a time, witness enters. Then jury]
Prosecutor: The delays in payment, put up the email

Stormy Daniels (reading) No funds have been received. My client says the deal is off unless funds received by 5 pm. -Keith. The ab initit, no idea what that means -
Prosecutor: Ad initio
Daniels: I spoke to Slate, they weren't going to pay me.

Prosecutor: This new agreement, did you sign it?

Stormy Daniels: Yes.
Prosecutor: And the side letter agreement?
Daniels: I signed it on Oct 28, 2016.
Prosecutor: Did Keith Davidson take a few? And Gina?
Daniels; Yes
Prosecutor: Did the WSJ reach out to you
A: No

Prosecutor: Was Mr. Trump elected?
Stormy Daniels: Yes.
Prosecutor: How was your 2017?
Daniels: Great, my best ever. I got a horse-riding award; my neighbors didn't know they lived next to Stormy Daniels, only Mom.
Prosecutor: What's this?
Daniels: Keith D's denial

Prosecutor: Was it cleverly misleading?
Objection!
Justice Merchan: Sustained.
Prosecutor: Did you see this 2018 story.
Stormy Daniels: It outed me. It hurt my daughter. Her father -
Objection!
Justice Merchan: Sustained

Prosecutor: Were you schedule to go on the Kimmel show?
Stormy Daniels: Yes. Gina brought me clothes - and Keith Davidson. He had another statement. I signed it as Stormy Daniels, but unlike any other time I signed. It was a tip off to Kimmel

Stormy Daniels: Michael Cohen was writing a book, it made me mad - he could talk about it and I couldn't.
Prosecutor: Did Michael Cohen file a TRO against you?
Daniels: Yes
Prosecutor: Did you hire Michael Avenatti?
Daniels: Yes. We canceled the NDA and got fees

Prosecutor: Your book "Full Disclosure," does it describe both the encounter with Mr. Trump and incidents in your childhood?
Stormy Daniels: Yes. I later found out that Michael Avenatti had dome some editing.
Prosecutor: Did Avenatti filed a defamation case?

Stormy Daniels: Yes but I hadn't agreed to it. I thought it was risky.

Prosecution: Did Avenatti put out a sketch regarding the 2011 threat? And Mr. Trump tweeted "con job"?

Daniels: Yes.

Prosecutor: Was Mr. Trump awarded legal fees?

Daniels: Yes.

Prosecutor: Is Mr. Avenatti your lawyer now?

Stormy Daniels: No. (Laughs). He is in jail.

Prosecutor: Have you paid the legal fees?

Daniels: No. I don't have the money, and I didn't think it was fair.

Prosecutor: Any relation to this case?

Daniels: No.

Prosecutor: Did you go on podcasts with Michael Cohen?

Stormy Daniels: Yes. I wanted to hear him apologize. And he did. Then we did one up to Michael Avenatti.

Prosecutor: Did you get $100,000 from a documentary?

Daniels: Yes.

[Now "Horseface" Truth shown, 408A]

[From the post: jail bird Michael Cohen. Sleaze bag]
Prosecutor: Has he called you sleazebag before?
Stormy Daniels: Yes.
Prosecutor: And is the post false?
Daniels: It is.
Prosecutor: No further questions.
Justice Merchan: Your witness...

Trump's lawyer Necheles: I represent President Trump. You've met with prosecutors & rehearsed your testimony?
Stormy Daniels: I didn't rehearse.
Necheles: You pretended to be cross examined, right?
Daniels: No.
Necheles: You said "mock"
Daniels: No longer right

Trump's lawyer Necheles: You said you did porno for more money, right?
Stormy Daniels: Don't we all. That's what we do here.
Necheles: You hate President Trump, right?
Daniels: Yes.
Necheles: You wrote you'll dance when he's

jailed?

Daniels: Can you show me that?

Trump's lawyer Necheles: You wrote, when he is selected to go to jail - did you just laugh?

Stormy Daniels: Someone else wrote select - it's funny.

Necheles: It's not because you think this is all funny?

Daniels: No.

Necheles: You owe him $500,000 in legal fees?

Stormy Daniels: I'm not sure of the dates.

Trump's lawyer Necheles: March 2022, you were ordered to pay attorney's fees for the appeal too, right?

Daniels: Yes

Necheles: More in 2023 because of your frivolous suit-

Prosecutor: Objection!

Justice Merchan: Sustained

Trump's lawyer Necheles: You have money, right?

Stormy Daniels: We all have money.

Necheles: You have said you will never pay, right?
Daniels: Correct
Necheles: I offer her tweet into evidence
Prosecution: Objection!
Justice Merchan: Sustained. Approach

[After sidebar]
Justice Merchan: Accepted into evidence.
[The tweet: "I will go to jail before I pay a penny."]
Trump's lawyer Necheles: That was you saying you didn't care about a Federal order, right?
Stormy Daniels: I won't pay for telling the truth.

Trump's lawyer Necheles: You wrote this, I don't owe him shit and I'll never give that orange turd a dime?
Stormy Daniels: Yes
Necheles: You make fun of how he looks too, right?
Daniels: He did it first
Necheles: You are refused to fill out an assets form?
A False

Trump's lawyer Necheles: Did you give an interview to Jeff Tubin and say you would not fill out the form?
Stormy Daniels: They asked about my daughter.
Necheles: Only her name. Let me show you J10-A. Recognize it?
Daniels: An email from my attorney

Trump's lawyer Necheles: You only partially filled it out right?
Prosecutor: Objection
Justice Merchan: Sustained
Necheles: May we approach, your Honor?
[Sidebar - Trump sits with Blanche at defense table]
Necheles: Show her page-
Justice Merchan: Take that down!

Trump's lawyer Necheles: Let me hand you this. It is only partially filled out - it asks income, you say Unknown, right?
Stormy Daniels: I won't fill out info that endangers my daughter.
Necheles: It asked what cars you own & you won't answer, right?
Daniels: Yeah

Trump's lawyer Necheles: You own a home?
Stormy Daniels: No.
Necheles: You tweeted you made so much in porn you could just buy your ranch home?
Daniels: We didn't buy it. I would have to see the tweet
Necheles: J-17

Trump's lawyer Necheles: You said, I just paid for my ranch-
Stormy Daniels: I meant, pay rent.
Necheles: Really. Are you making money claiming to have had sex for more than a decade, right?
Daniels: I make money telling my story. It also costs me money

Trump's lawyer Necheles: Didn't you speak with Gloria Allred?
Stormy Daniels: I told her I had sex with Donald Trump..
Necheles: Is this your book Full Disclosure?
Daniels: Yes.
Necheles: You say Gina Rodriguez set up a call with Gloria Allred
A: Yes.

Trump's lawyer Necheles: You told Gloria Allred you did not have sex with President Trump, right?
Stormy Daniels: No - I told her I did have sex with him.
Necheles: Let me show you - you say, you left out sex
Daniels: Later I told her
Necheles: Not in the book

Stormy Daniels: I would not go with force so I said no.
Trump's lawyer Necheles: You're just making this up now, aren't you?
Daniels: I didn't trust her.

Trump's lawyer Necheles: It taught you if you want to make money off President Trump, you have to claim scx?
Daniels: No. But it seems to be that way.
Necheles: When you spoke with In Touch, you were trying to sell your story, right?
Daniels: Yes.

Trump's lawyer Necheles: At the same time you were telling In Touch you had sex with President Trump, while threatening to sue

The Dirty Dot Com to take it down.
Stormy Daniels: The Dirty dot com happened after the parking lot threat
Necheles: Are you sure?

Trump's lawyer Necheles: You were saying it was bullsh*t, while getting paid $15,000 to say it was true-
Stormy Daniels: I did Anderson Cooper and they didn't pay me anything!
Necheles: We'll get to that. The In Touch was a 22-page transcript. In 15 minutes?

Trump's lawyer Necheles: After the threat you went to exercise class?
Stormy Daniels: I went to the restroom there, waited for the next class. I was crying in the bathroom but I said my daughter had a diaper blow-up.
Necheles: This the first time you say crying

Stormy Daniels: I did say she had a blowout [she gestures at jury]
Trump's lawyer Necheles: You didn't even tell the father of your baby right?
Daniels: I didn't.
Necheles: You said nothing until 7 years

later? With your daughter in danger?
SD: Right

Trump's lawyer Necheles: You made up this threat to explain why you never said you had sex with President Trump, right?
Stormy Daniels: No. I said it on a radio station in Tampa.
Necheles: You told Anderson Cooper you'd never said it before
Daniels: I was scared

Trump's lawyer Necheles: Both you and Michael Cohen hope to make money if President Trump, right?
Prosecution: Objection!
Justice Merchan: Sustained.
Necheles: You commissioned a sketch of the threatener?
A: Avenatti did

Necheles: Shall we take a break?
Justice Merchan: Yes.

[They're back - and, Stormy will still be on the stand Thursday]
Trump's lawyer Necheles: In E you were

quoted, The story is bullsh*t - but didn't you say he vehemently deny to E hooking up with President Trump?
Stormy Daniels; I do not remember that.

Trump's lawyer Necheles: You're saying that where the article says you vehemently deny the story, that's false?
Stormy Daniels: Yes!
Necheles: You told the Dirty to take it down
Daniels: I didn't do it.. Keith did. He was Gina's lawyer. I authorized him to down it

Trump's lawyer Necheles: In 2011 the story wasn't worth much - but then it was worth more in 2016, right?
Stormy Daniels: I set a free press conference.
Necheles: But you never held it. You say you were threatened if you spoke, so you spoke
Daniels: New ballgame

Trump's lawyer Necheles: In this text, Gina said, I have Stormy Daniels. Please read Dylan Howard
Stormy Daniels: denounced it previously - I don't want to comment if I don't understand what they are talking about

Necheles: "She had sex with him. She wants $100K"

Stormy Daniels: I authorized Gina Rodriguez to shop the story. I wanted to get the story out and make some money too.
Justice Merchan: We'll end here

Chapter 10: Stormy Daniels Disclaims Name of Strip Dancing Tour as Is Shown Nasty Tweets

On the second day of Stormy Daniels in the Trump Trial, defense lawyer Susan Necheles asked about her "Make America Horny" tour and whether her boyfriend of the time had thought she'd lost her mind.

As to the tour, Daniels said she hadn't named it, and didn't like the name. Questions about attacks by and apparently on the ex-boyfriend were excluded by Justice Merchan.

Defense lawyer Todd Blanche, who sat chatting with Trump during many of the sidebars, ended the morning by saying he would be moving to exclude Karen McDougal's testimony, after again moving for a mistrial based on Daniels. It was set for 4 pm.

Necheles compared the witness' story now in 2024 to what she told InTouch magazine in 2011. Not just whether she felt threatened - then and now, she said no - but whether she and Trump had had dinner.

Where I come from, Daniels answered, you can have dinner without putting anything in your mouth.

Some opined that Necheles had gone on too long on cross, and paradoxically turned it into a rape case. But if not a mistrial, could this all get any conviction reversed, a la

Harvey Weinstein? As Daniels was on redirect shown nasty tweets it was reminiscent of E. Jean Carroll v. Trump just down that street in SDNY

Chapter 11: Court Artist

I try to capture Trump not in orange
But how I feel him, he greets me
His base, I'll be sure to note, threatens me
Just like Tom Brady's, maybe it's related

The only time I cried with Susan Smith
She killed her babies and I had one that age
I once drew an execution
And then another, George Floyd

Others stay more quiet
But I work in bright colors
Just don't come at me
With that MAGA red....

Chapter 12: Stormy II - pearl Necklace

Thinks she's so smart
The orange man's gray sword

Performing as surely as I did
While trying to shame me
Good luck, pearl Necklace

Chapter 13: May 9, 2024 Trump Trial Day

Trump comes in, blue suit and blue tie, chats with Todd Blanche to his left. Susan Necheles, mid-cross of Stormy is in the lead counsel's chair today - Trump turns and talks to her, gesturing with his right hand. Waiting for Justice Merchan. Drum roll...

All rise!
Clerk: This is the People of the State of New York versus Donald J. Trump!
Justice Merchan: Good morning.
Prosecutor: There is a defendant exhibit, J26, an arrest record of Ms. Daniels. We move to preclude that.
Justice Merchan: No conviction?
Trump's lawyer Necheles: I plan to ask her about what her ex-husband accused her of -

Justice Merchan: No, it's not coming in. Where do you stand on a limiting instruction?
Necheles: Can we wait to the end of testimony?
Justice Merchan: Yes. Get the witness, please

[Stormy Daniels takes the stand]
Justice Merchan: Get the jury, please.
Clerk: All rise! Jury entering!
Trump's lawyer Susan Necheles: Ms. Daniels, you recall that President Trump was elected in November 2016?
Stormy Daniels: Correct

Trump's lawyer Necheles: You recall you did an interview and said the claims you had sex with President Trump was bullshit -
Prosecutor: Objection!
Justice Merchan: Sustained.
Necheles: But do you remember?
Justice Merchan: Sustained!

Trump's lawyer Necheles: In 2016, then, you wanted to sell you story. You -
Justice Merchan: Please approach.
[Whispered sidebar ensues - Blanche remains

at defense table with Trump, also whispering]
Justice Merchan: The objection is sustained.

Trump's lawyer Necheles: You wanted to sell your story to President Trump, right?
Stormy Daniels: No, I wanted to sell my story to the media, to get my story out.
Necheles: You made the decision for your lawyers to sell it - your choice, right?

Stormy Daniels: I wanted to do a press conference.
Trump's lawyer Necheles: But you didn't. You spoke to Slate's Weisberg about your supposed affair with President Trump, and that you were negotiating with Cohen, right?
Daniels: He was my back-up

Trump's lawyer Necheles: Look at this exhibit [not in evidence - yet?] you told Weisberg that as an alternative to being paid for your silence you wanted to be paid for your story, right?
Daniels: I don't remember saying that.
Necheles: But you told Weisberg that

Stormy Daniels: The better alternative was to get my story protected by a paper trial w/o

putting my family at risk.
Trump's lawyer Necheles: You told Weisberg that your motive was President Trump having come out against gay marriage and abortion?
Daniels: False

Trump's lawyer Necheles: Put up the transcript, already in evidence
[Voice of Keith Davidson, heard before in this trial]
Prosecutor: Objection.
Justice Merchan: Sustained. Please approach
[Sidebar]

[After sidebar, Necheles plays another clip in evidence]
Trump's lawyer Necheles: Let me show you the contract - you know it's a legal agreement, right?
Stormy Daniels: I'm not an attorney but yes.
Necheles: The recitals says, you had come into confidential info

Stormy Daniels: I signed this based on what my attorney said I should do.
Trump's lawyer Necheles: But you signed it, you released claims, right?

Daniels: Yes.
Necheles: Michael Cohen negotiated it, right?
Daniels: That's what I was led to believe

Trump's lawyer Necheles: Here is the WSJ article - you knew it was coming out, right?
Stormy Daniels: Keith Davidson told me something was coming out.
Necheles: And you put up a statement denying you had sex with President Trump, right? [Reads it]

Stormy Daniels: I didn't write it. I was told I had to sign it.
Trump's lawyer Necheles: You denied the rumor-
Daniels: Because it wasn't a rumor. It was true.
Necheles: You signed this, too, on January 30, 2018, right?
Daniels: Yes.

Trump's lawyer Necheles: Michael Cohen was pushing you to sign this?
Stormy Daniels: Though Keith Davidson. I did not speak with Michael Cohen directly.
Necheles: President Trump was denying the

affair in 2018 - he was not running for office, right?

Trump's lawyer Necheles: President Trump was trying to protect his brand, right?
Stormy Daniels: I don't know what he was trying to protect.
Necheles: Then you said you had sex with him, to make money?
Daniels: I did some media for free. Anderson Cooper

Trump's lawyer Necheles: But after that you sold a book with your story for $800,000 right?
Stormy Daniels: Yes. But I also didn't receive the $800,000.
Necheles: But so far it came to $930,000, right?
Daniels: Minus what was stolen from me.

Trump's lawyer Necheles: After the book you went on a strip tour called "Make America Horny"?
Stormy Daniels: I did not name the tour. I fought it tooth and nail.
Necheles: You advertised your tour with the

photo from the golf tournament, right?
Daniels: Not me

Trump's lawyer Necheles: Didn't you say the white men were gone, now your fan based as gay couples and the Resistance?
Stormy Daniels: It did change. But I was not selling myself.
Necheles: You were selling a story of supposedly have sex with Donald Trump, right?

Trump's lawyer Necheles: You made $200,000 for appearing on The Surreal Life, right?
Stormy Daniels: Yes.
Necheles: And a documentary on TV? You were paid for the rights to your book, right?
Daniels: They didn't have to.
Necheles: You had sex with a cameraman?

Stormy Daniels: I started dating him and he became my husband.
Trump's lawyer Necheles: But you were married at the time, right?
Daniels: I was separated.
Necheles: Where did you deposit the money?

Daniels: Into my business account. It covers my security.

Trump's lawyer Necheles: At the viewing parties, you are treated like a hero? They say, you are saving America?
Stormy Daniels: That's in strip clubs. The viewing parties are polarizing.
Necheles: You said you'll be instrumental in putting President Trump in jail?

Stormy Daniels: Show me where I said instrumental.
Trump's lawyer Necheles: Here's your tweet, "Making me the best person to flush the orange turd down."
Daniels: It doesn't say Trump, just orange turd. If you want to interpret it that way...

Trump's lawyer Necheles: I offer your tweet -
Stormy Daniels: It's to a suspended account, so I don't know.
Prosecutor: I object, your Honor. May we approach?
[Whispered sidebar; at defense table, again, Todd Blanche whispering to Trump]

Trump's lawyer Necheles: On Twitter you celebrated and tried to sell merchandise in your online store, right? You have a store?
Stormy Daniels: Sure.
Necheles: You wrote, Don't want to spill my champagne, merch orders pouring in, right
Daniels: Yes

Trump's lawyer Necheles: This was you shilling your merch, right?
Stormy Daniels: I am doing my job. Not unlike Mr. Trump.
Necheles: Your merchandise is you bragging getting President Trump indicted, right?
Daniels: *I* got President Trump indicted?

Trump's lawyer Necheles: You're making $40 for every "Stormy Saint of Indictments" candle?
Stormy Daniels: I only make about $7 per.
Necheles: Here's the Stormy Daniels Political Power comic?
Daniels: I didn't write it
Necheles: But you're selling it?
Daniels: Yes

Trump's lawyer Necheles: You're writing two books - what are they about?
Stormy Daniels: Rock Star, Porn Star about my husband. And a novel about a girl from New Orleans.
Necheles: Does she have sex with a presidential candidate?
Daniels: No

Trump's lawyer Necheles: You said that you lived in a haunted house in New Orleans where a ghost held your husband under water?
Stormy Daniels: Some was a possum under the house.
Necheles: I ask to strike that
Justice Merchan: Overruled.

Trump's lawyer Necheles: Didn't you attack your boyfriend?
Prosecutor: Objection - we talked about this.
Justice Merchan: Yes. Move on.
Necheles: But didn't your boyfriend question your sanity?
Prosecutor: Objection!

Trump's lawyer Necheles: You've been in over 200 sex films?
Stormy Daniels: Including comps.
Necheles: What?
Daniels: Compilations.
Necheles: So you have experience in making up fake stories about sex?
Daniels: The sex is real. That's why it's not a B movie.

Trump's lawyer Necheles: Now you have a story about having sex with President Trump, right?
Stormy Daniels: If I was making it up it would have been a lot better.
Necheles: You make money working in the sex clubs-
Daniels: I work in strip clubs, big difference.

Trump's lawyer Necheles: Remember Ms. Hoffinger asking if you remembered the black and white tiled floor, right?
Stormy Daniels: There is nothing wrong with preparing a witness. I would hope any lawyer would do that.
Necheles: It was to match your book, right?

Trump's lawyer Necheles: This supposed sex took place 18 years ago, right? And only you and President Trump were supposedly there?
Stormy Daniels: And his bodyguard, right at the door.
Necheles: You say you met in Lake Tahoe?
Daniels: Yes

Trump's lawyer Necheles: There were a lot celebrities at the golf tournament - Aaron Rogers, right?
Stormy Daniels: I don't know.
Necheles: Charles Barkley?
Daniels: Yes.
Necheles: Your picture with President Trump was one of dozens of photos you took, right?
Yes

Trump's lawyer Necheles: Your testimony is that you told Keith Schiller, F*ck no. But you gave him your number?
Stormy Daniels: Right
Necheles: But in 2011 you told InTouch magazine differently, didn't you? Show J-23. You said President Trump asked for your number

Trump's lawyer Necheles: You said you rode on a golf cart together & you gave your number to President Trump?
Stormy Daniels: I gave it to his bodyguard
Necheles: But you didn't mention his bodyguard to InTouch
Daniels: They tried to get me to not mention others

Trump's lawyer Necheles: But here in the story you do mention Keith Schiller... In 2011 you told the interviewer you said, to dinner, Yeah, of course.
Stormy Daniels: My publicist told me that. This is a frivolous entertainment magazine.
Necheles: So you lied

Trump's lawyer Necheles: You told Kimmel, We never had dinner, he lied to me. I stayed for the food. You said that?
Stormy Daniels: I was invited to dinner and I never got dinner. I am very food motivated.
Necheles: J-28, page 4.
Daniels: Where is this from? Oh

Trump's lawyer Necheles: On Anderson Cooper in 2018, you said you had dinner with

President Trump?
Stormy Daniels: I'd like to be shown what I said.
Necheles: You remember the tiles on the floor but not this?
Prosecutor: Objection!
Justice Merchan: Sustained.

Trump's lawyer Necheles: You said you had dinner but you didn't
Stormy Daniels: Where I come from having dinner doesn't necessarily mean putting food in your mouth
Necheles: You said President Trump sent a car
Daniels: I don't know who sent it. It was before Uber

Trump's lawyer Necheles: You told InTouch magazine that when you got to the hotel President Trump was sprawled out on the couch watching TV, right?
Stormy Daniels: I don't remember saying that.
Necheles: You said "sprawled out in pajama pants"
Daniels: He got up

Trump's lawyer Necheles: In your book you wrote that you had made him your bitch, right? Because you are powerful.
Stormy Daniels: I used to think so.
Necheles: This was not the first time someone made a pass at you?
Daniels: There was a bodyguard out there

Trump's lawyer Necheles: In 2011 you told InTouch that when you saw him on the bed you said, Oh, here we go and then started kissing and had sex, right?
Stormy Daniels: There are parts I don't remember in between.

[Trump is leaning forward, watching this closely]
Trump's lawyer Necheles: In InTouch it doesn't have him saying, If you want to get what you want, and trailer park
Stormy Daniels: They left out a lot of stuff.

Trump's lawyer Necheles: You were interviews for Slate magazine in 2018 by Jacob Weisberg-
Stormy Daniels: I don't know if that was his name. That's what it says.

Necheles: You told Mr. Weisberg there was no abuse, you were not a victim?
Daniels: Right

Trump's lawyer Necheles: You never told Weisberg about blacking out
Stormy Daniels: No. Mr. Trump did not drug me. The worst thing he did was lie.
Necheles: In 2018, you said he didn't force you - but Tuesday you said he stood over you-
Daniels: In front of me

Trump's lawyer Necheles: In 2018 you told a reporter there was no pressure
Stormy Daniels: My own insecurities made me do it.
Necheles: The American Century Championship had parties and auctions
Daniels: There were a couple of auctions

Trump's lawyer Necheles: In your book you said at the nightclub you talked with President Trump for an hour
Stormy Daniels: He left first, after about 15 minutes
Necheles: In 2007 you took a selfie in Trump

Tower, that's it?
Daniels: Also at the Trump Vodka party

Justice Merchan: Let's take our morning break.

They're back.
Trump's lawyer Necheles: Do you recognize this Making American Horny tour flier from your Instagram?
Stormy Daniels: Yes
Necheles: At the golf tournament, President Trump was probably the biggest celebrity?
Daniels: Depends. People recognized me too

Trump's lawyer Necheles: When Vogue interviewed you in 2018 you said you never felt in danger, he wouldn't have run after you- you didn't mention the bodyguard?
Stormy Daniels: I don't control it. Vogue is a fashion magazine. Sometimes I give too much details.

Trump's lawyer Necheles: Mr. Cohen paid you, not Mr. Trump, right?
Stormy Daniels: My lawyer Keith Davidson

paid me.

Necheles: But the money was from Mr. Cohen

Daniels: I understand that, but I have no proof.

Necheles: You know this is a business records indictment?

Stormy Daniels: There are a lot of indictments.

Necheles: Move to strike

Justice Merchan: Overruled.

Necheles: No further questions.

Prosecutor: Can we have a sidebar?

Justice Merchan: Yes. Approach.

[This time it's Emil Bove who stays with Trump at defense table, chatting. On the witness stand, Stormy Daniels put his chin on her fist]

[They've back, for re-direct]

Prosecutor: You were asked if fear was part of your reason for signing the NDA

Trump's lawyer Necheles: Objection!

Justice Merchan: Overruled

Prosecutor: Your lawyer advised you to sign

it?

Stormy Daniels: He said, Get high, stay high

Prosecutor: There was no lawsuit pending when you signed the NDA, right?

Stormy Daniels: There was not

Prosecutor: Put up People's 171A [text messages] "Is she ready to talk?" Dylan said, "I thought she denounced it previously." She asked you to read that, right

Prosecutor: But she didn't ask you to read the very next box, where Gina's says she - you - never did, right?

Stormy Daniels: She didn't.

Prosecutor: And the InTouch says Lightly edited - did she ask you about that?

Daniels: No.

Prosecutor: You didn't tell every single detail to Anderson Cooper, did you?

Stormy Daniels: I did not.

[A sidebar is called, after which]

Justice Merchan: Ms. Hoffinger you may clarify to the extent we discussed.

Prosecutor Hoffinger: You told Anderson Cooper you had sex with Mr. Trump & what

happened in the room
Trump's lawyer Necheles: Objection!
Justice Merchan: Overruled. Please approach.
[Side bar, then]
Prosecutor: You told Anderson Cooper a lot
Stormy Daniels: I did

Prosecutor: When you said you would celebrate when Mr. Trump was selected, were you responding to being called disgusting prostitute?
Stormy Daniels: Yes
Prosecutor: When Mr. Trump posted If you go after me, I'm coming after you- was it you?
Daniels: I thought so

Prosecutor: You didn't testify to the grand jury in this case, did you?
Trump's lawyer Necheles: Objection!
Justice Merchan: Overruled.
Stormy Daniels: I did not.
Prosecutor: In Mr. Trump's lawyer's papers in 2017 he confirmed Michael Cohen was reimbursed?
A: Yes

Prosecutor: Has your telling the truth about what happened with Mr. Trump been net positive or net negative in your life?
Trump's lawyer Necheles: Objection!
Justice Merchan: Overruled.
Stormy Daniels: Net negative.
Prosecutor: Nothing further

Justice Merchan: Re-cross.
Trump's lawyer Necheles: These things happen on Twitter right, receiving nasty messages from your political opponents?
Stormy Daniels: Yes.
Necheles: You wrote that you'll dance down the street "when he is 'selected' to go to jail"

Trump's lawyer Necheles: You were called an aging harlot - nasty, right? And you jabbed back and said you made a million dollars and just paid for your new ranch
Stormy Daniels: Yes I defend myself on Twitter. And I pay my bills.

Trump's lawyer Necheles: When President Trump posted "I'm coming after you," there was a Republican PAC going after President Trump, right?

Stormy Daniels: I don't know.
Necheles: No further questions.
Justice Merchan: Nothing further? You may step down.

Prosecutor: The People call Rebecca Manochio... Where do you work?
Manochio: At the Trump Organization. For 11 years. I am a bookkeeper there. I worked at supermarket, then the Trump Organization.
Prosecutor: Who is the head of it?
Manochio: Donald Trump.

Prosecutor: Who is Jeff McConney?
Manochio: The controller.
Prosecutor: What is a controller?
Manochio: I don't really know.
Prosecutor: Did you also work for Mr. Weisselberg?
Manochio: Yes. I sat just outside his office. I handled invoices.

Prosecutor: Did Mr. Trump get a new job in 2016?
Manochio: Yes.
Prosecutor: Did he have to move?
Manochio: Yes.

Prosecutor: To where?
Manochio: The White House.
Prosecutor: How then did he get his checks to sign?
Manochio: Deb Terasoff gave to me, I FedExed them

Prosecutor: How many would you sent at one time?
Manochio: Between 10 and 20
Prosecutor: Did you ever send a single check?
Manochio: Yes.
Prosecutor: Did you include a return FedEx envelope, addressed to you?
Manochio: Yes.

Prosecutor: If a check was missing who would you contact?
Manochio: Madeleine Westerhout.
Prosecutor: Have you reviewed the documents on the thumb drive?
Manochio: Yes.
Prosecutor: Display PX 291 [FedEx invoice of May 29, 2017]

Prosecutor: Who did you send these checks to?

Manochio: Keith Schiller's home address in DC.
Prosecutor: Did there come a time Mr. Schiller left?
Manochio: Yes.
Prosecutor: Then you sent to John McEntee?
Manochio: Yes.

Prosecutor: Is this from Mr. McEntee to you?
Manochio: Yes. Signed checks.
Prosecutor: No further questions.
Justice Merchan: We'll take lunch.

Interim programming note:
After jury left, Trump's lawyer Todd Blanche said they want to move again for a mistrial, and if that fails, to preclude the testimony of Karen McDougal.
Justice Merchan said that'll be at 4 pm.
Thread will resume 2:10 or so

They've back, Trump talking to Emil Bove while Blanche and Susan Necheles stand.
Now the prosecutors arrive
All rise!

Justice Merchan: Let's get the witness please. And jury.

Trump's lawyer Necheles: You also sent Ivanka Trump's checks?

Manochio: Yes. The same way

Trump's lawyer Necheles: Do you know if it took the White House a long time to process mail and get it to President Trump?

Manochio: I don't know.

Necheles: Do you know if that's why the checks were sent to people?

Prosecutor: Objection

Justice Merchan: Sustained

Trump's lawyer Necheles: By then, President Trump was not speaking with Allen Weisselberg at all?

Manochio: He was not.

Necheles: No further questions.

No re-direct

Justice Merchan: Next witness.

Tracy Menzies, of Harper Collins.

Prosecutor: At Harper Collins, how involved are authors in the production of their books?

Menzies: We work with them - they are fully

engaged.

Prosecutor: Are you familiar with "Think Big" by Donald Trump and Bill Zanker?
Menzies: Yes.

Prosecutor: When was it first published?
Menzies: 2007. This edition is from 2021.
Prosecutor: Can you tell which author wrote which section?
Menzies: Yes. Different fonts.
[Half redacted page shown to jury]
Menzies: This is by Mr. Trump, "Don't Trust Anyone"

Prosecutor: What's this?
Menzies: Mr. Trump writes, I value loyalty, we reward it, people like Allen Weisselberg. "I just can't stomach disloyalty... When someone screw you, screw them back in spades. Getting even is part of doing business."
Prosecutor: No more Qs

Trump's lawyer Todd Blanche: Those pages were redacted. The book is 300 pages, you were shown six, right?
Menzies: Right.

Blanche: Did President Trump thank Meredith McIver?
Menzies: Yes.
Blanche: Could each author have had help?
Menzies: Yes.
Next witness

Prosecutor: The People call Madeleine Westerhout. Where do you work?
Westerhout: A geo-political consulting firm. I work for the CEO.
Prosecutor: Whose paying for your lawyer?
Westerhout: He graciously agreed to do it pro bono.
Prosecutor: Where did you work?

Westerhout: The RNC.
Prosecutor: How long?
Westerhout: 2013 to 2017.
Prosecutor: Did you become aware of the Access Hollywood tape - what impact on RNC leadership?
Westerhout: There were conversations about replacing Mr. Trump as the candidate

Prosecutor: Did you spend time at Trump Tower?

Westerhout: Yes. On Jan 20, 2017, I was taken to my desk, right outside the Oval Office.

Prosecutor: Did anyone else sit closer to the President?

Westerhout: Hope Hicks. Also John McEntee and Keith Schiller

Prosecutor: How does someone call the President?

Westerhout: They might call me. Or the Situation Room. If it was John Smith off the street, there were screeners.

Prosecutor: Did Mr. Trump use a computer or have an email account?

Westerhout: Not to my knowledge.

Prosecutor: Would he pay attention to detail?

Westerhout: Yes. He signed things himself with a Sharpie.

Prosecutor: Did you use social media?

Westerhout: Twitter, now X. As RealDonaldTrump

Prosecutor: Did anyone else have access?

Westerhout: Dan Scavino

Westerhout: Sometime the President would dictate a Tweet to me, I'd type it up and print it out for him to review. There were certain words he liked to capitalize, like COUNTRY. And he used exclamation points and the Oxford comma.

Prosecutor: Did you coordinate with the Trump Organization?
Westerhout: Sometimes. With Rhona Graff.
Prosecutor: On his contacts and calendar and mail?
Westerhout: Yes.
[Trump is whispering to Susan Necheles. Looks like she'll cross examine]

Prosecutor: Please read this email.
Westerhout: I asked Rhona Graff, can the girls get together a list of people he usually speaks with... then smiley face.
Prosecutor: On this list, who is David Pecker?
Westerhout: A tabloid person

Prosecutor: Did you think Michael Cohen and Mr. Trump has a close relationship in 2017?
Westerhout: At that time they did.
Prosecutor: What's this?

Westerhout: An email I sent to Michael Cohen at Trump Org before he came to the White House.

Prosecutor: What's this?
Westerhout: My texts with Hope Hicks, I asked her "Hey the president want to know if you called David pecker again?"
Prosecutor: And this?
Westerhout: Mail between Rebecca Manochio and Keith Schiller.

Prosecutor: Do you know what the WInged Foot Golf Club is?
Westerhout: I believe it's a golf course. This is about his annual dues. President Trump wrote PAY ASAP.
Prosecutor: And this?
Westerhout: Rhona wrote to me about getting a frame from Tiffany's next door

Westerhout: Rhona Graff said the frame cost $650 minus a 15% discount and should she get it.
Prosecutor: Did Mr. Trump usually get involved in things like this?

Westerhout: Not usually. But this was a frame for a photo of his mother.

Prosecutor: Describe Melania's and Mr. Trump's relationship.
Westerhout: I thought it was special. He'd have me call her and say he was running late, just like any other marriage.

Prosecutor: How did you leave the White House?
Westerhout: I went to what I thought was an off the record dinner and said some things I shouldn't have and I lost my job, I regret my youthful indiscretion [sobs]
Prosecutor: Do you need a moment?
No

Prosecutor: Why did you write your book?
Westerhout: I wanted my family to know, and I wanted people to know the man I got to know, I don't think he is treated fairly [wipes eyes]
Prosecutor: Did you speak with him?
Westerhout: At a fundraiser in NJ
No more Qs

Trump's lawyer Necheles [at 3:48] Shall we break here?

Justice Merchan: No, we'll go to 4 pm.

Necheles: You thought President Trump was good President?

Westerhout: Yes.

Necheles: President Trump kept moving forward, didn't freak out, right?

Westerhout: He did.

Trump's lawyer Necheles: After he won he had to interview people - and you worked on the briefing papers?

Westerhout: I did.

Necheles: When they called you the greeter girl it was belittling by the press, right, as the prosecutor asked you?

Westerhout: Yes.

Westerhout: He never made me feel I didn't deserve to be in the White House.

Trump's lawyer Necheles: He had a close relationship with his wife?

Westerhout: I'd look into the Oval and see he was talking to Melania, he'd say, Some to the window and they'd wave

Trump's lawyer Necheles: Is this a good time to break?

Justice Merchan: Yes.

[Jurors leave. Then:] Let's take 10 min then pick it up

They've back - with news:

Trump's lawyer Todd Blanche: We have been informed the People no longer intend to call Karen McDougal as a witness.

Trump's lawyer Blanche: They now have only one major witness, Michael Cohen. We ask that the gag order be lifted as to Stormy Daniels. Her Lake Tahoe friend went on a political show. He needs to be able to respond.

Justice Merchan: Let me hear from the People

Prosecutor: The other side seems to be in an alternate reality. The gag order has been to protect this proceeding, and it has been working. This defendant mounts attacks, selfishly. There are safety concerns.

Prosecutor: Changing the gag order now could send a message to other witnesses. The DC Circuit said, "it is likely to impact other witnesses." I was speaking with a custodial witness who was afraid. His book said, attack to send a message.

Trump's lawyer Blanche: Ms. Daniels was allowed to recount a completely different set of events -
Justice Merchan: Such as?
Blanche: She said, I felt the room spin - what she had previously said "here we go, we started kissing, I hope he doesn't try to pay me."

Trump's lawyer Blanche: Now she said, I blacked out -
Justice Merchan: I don't see a new sct of facts. Please have a seat. What Mr. Conroy said, it's interesting, I wrote down the same potion of the book, let others see

Justice Merchan: I can't take your word for it that it's just going to be a response, disputing the facts. That's not your client's track record. Your application to modify the gag order to allow your client to respond to Ms. Daniels is denied.

Trump's lawyer Blanche: The government got her to talk about spanking him - they did not move on. There was a question asked about what the inside of the bathroom looked like inside - why? And What was your reaction to seeing him like that? There was a long answer

Trump's lawyer Blanche: They asked her what was the difference in height - why? She said, There was an imbalance of power for sure - it doesn't go to motive, she wasn't saying it at the time. There was no basis to ask. We heard all this for the first time

Justice Merchan: I sustained some objections.
Trump's lawyer Blanche: But the jury still heard the question and often the answer.
That's why this was so dangerous. This was a dog whistle for rape.
Prosecutor: So much is false

Prosecutor: The claim of ambush is nonsense. OK there were details omitted from InTouch, but in Anderson Cooper. This is not a change of story. Ms. Necheles' thorough but misleading cross tested it. That the sex happened increases the motivation to silence her

Prosecutor: We went out of our way to avoid some of the salacious details, to not embarrass the defendant with the details of the sexual act. At one point she was asked did you feel anything difference. She was going to say, I felt the skin of a 60-year-old man

Prosecutor: We could put in an ex parte submission of more embarrassing details we omitted, to not embarrass the defendant. Ms. McDougal was on our witness list but we never said we intended to call her

Justice Merchan: Mr. Blanche, sit down so I can render my ruling. You denied the sexual encounter in your opening - so more details were relevant. Ms. Necheles said she thought she couldn't object, under my ruling. But she could have and didn't.

Justice Merchan: I sua sponte objected to the trailer park - Ms. Necheles hadn't objected. She didn't object to the condom - I have no idea why. I wish that hadn't come in. Then you went into it all, about force, on cross. Drilling it into the jurors' ears.

Justice Merchan: Ms. Daniels said a movie about Roger Ailes made her remember things. I didn't allow that. I don't think there is a new story here. You attacked her credibility in opening - you didn't attack the business records issues. Your motion is denied.

Justice Merchan: I'll see you tomorrow.

Chapter 14: Madeleine Westerhout

Why'd I have to go shoot
My big mouth off
About Don and Junior
Thinking I was one of them?

Then my desk cleaned out
There by the Resolute
They're resolute
The disloyal are dissed
And yet he hugged me
At a Jersey fundraiser
I'm crying

Chapter 15: May 10, 2024 Trump Trial Day

Trump is here, blue suit, red tie.
All rise!
Justice Merchan: Good morning Mr. Trump. Yesterday we have a witness on the stand. Anything we need to discuss?
Prosecutor: With permission, may we approach?
Justice Merchan: Yes
[Sidebar - Blanche stays with Trump]

[Sidebar continues; Trump at defense table showing his lawyer Todd Blanche some papers. Then:]
Justice Merchan: Let's get the witness, please.... Welcome back. Let's get the jury, please
Jury entering!
Trump's lawyer Necheles: You were at the

RNC?
Westerhout: Yes

Trump's lawyer Necheles: Would the RNC create a travel schedule for presumptive nominee Trump?
Westerhout: Yes.
Necheles: I want to show you L-8 and L-9. Oh, when they're ready. So People's 69 [the Trump contact list]

Trump's lawyer Necheles: You sent out this photo of the first time President Trump boarded Air Force One - he was proud, right?
Westerhout: Yes, he was proud.
Necheles: He often sent newspaper clippings to people?
Westerhout: He did.

Trump's lawyer Necheles: But only once to Allen Weisselberg?
Westerhout: It could have been.
Necheles: And he barely spoke to Allen Weisselberg in that first year, right?
Westerhout: Right
Necheles: I want to show you-

Prosecutor: Objection! Can we approach? Yes

[Long sidebar. Then:]
Trump's lawyer Necheles: Do you recognize this travel schedule?
Westerhout: I saw them when I was at RNC.
Necheles: They were created and kept in the ordinary court of the RNC's business, right?
Westerhout: Yes.
Prosecutor: May I voir dire?

Then:
Prosecutor: We object [to admission of RNC travel schedule into evidence. Sidebar ensues]
Justice Merchan: The motion to introduce this into evidence is denied.
Trump's lawyer Necheles: You were asked about how checks were sent, right?
Westerhout: Yes.

Trump's lawyer Necheles: At some point you were told that there was a post office box set up for the President and his wife to receive personal items?
Westerhout: Yes.

Necheles: But it was slow and things got lost?
Westerhout: Yes.

Trump's lawyer Necheles: President Trump was upset because he thought it was disrespectful if he didn't respond promptly?
Westerhout: Definitely.
Necheles: So things would be sent to Keith Schiller, right?
Westerhout: Right.

Trump's lawyer Necheles: Is it your understanding that this work-around happened in previous Administrations?
Westerhout: I can't imagine it would have been any different.
Necheles: You didn't give packages to Ivanka Trump?
Westerhout: I didn't.

Trump's lawyer Necheles: He signed a lot of things. He felt if people were getting his signature they should get his real signature, right?
Justice Merchan: Sustained. Stricken from the record.

Necheles: He signed checks while on the phone?
Westerhout: Yes.

Trump's lawyer Necheles: He was a person who multi-tasked, right?
Westerhout: Definitely.
Necheles: People's 75 [Email of Rhona Graff asking about buying photo frame at TIffany's] You said you made the executive decision to spend the money because he was busy?
Yes

Trump's lawyer Necheles: You were working in the White House when Stormy Daniels' story came out?
Westerhout: Yes.
Necheles: He was upset?
Westerhout: Yes. He was concerned his family would see it.
Justice Merchan: Sustained. The answer is stricken. Any redirect?

Prosecutor: You did not meet Mr. Trump personally until after the election, right?
Westerhout: Yes. November 2016.

Prosecutor: At Trump Tower did you sit on a different floor than President Trump?
Westerhout: Yes.

Prosecutor: Ms. Necheles didn't ask if you'd spoken before. Have you?
Westerhout: Once.
Prosecutor: When?
Westerhout: This week.
Prosecutor: Do you work at American Political Strategies, for Robert O'Brien, who worked in the Trump Administration?
Westerhout: Yes

Prosecutor: No further questions.
Re-cross
Trump's lawyer Necheles: Again, you testified that President Trump was very close with his family and-
Justice Merchan: Sustained. Stricken. Next witness.
Prosecutor: The People call Daniel Dixon. Where do you work?
AT&T

Prosecutor: What do you do there?
Dixon: Respond to legal demands, help law enforcement interpretate [sic] call records.
Prosecutor: Did you review this thumb drive?
Dixon: Yes. There are 6 AT&T numbers & 11 others.
Prosecutor: PX 400. Subject to sealing order

[On the screen: A Michael Cohen account report, with a dot DonaldTrump dot com email address. fwiw this witness Dixon is wearing a hat]
Prosecutor: What is a mobility report?
Dixon: Cell phone to cell phone.

Prosecutor: And this is how was can tell how the records work?
Dixon: Yes.
Prosecutor: No further questions.
Trump's lawyer Bove: A cross market move is a change in ATT's accounting?
Dixon: Yes
Bove: So this Michael Cohen move, it begins Jan 2017?
Dixon: Zoom out

Trump's lawyer Bove: You're aware of pocket dialing, yes?
Dixon: I am...
Bove: Nothing further.
Justice Merchan: Next witness.
Prosecutor: The People call Jenny Tomalin - of Verizon...

Prosecutor: Does Verizon keep call records?
Tomalin: Yes.
[Now put on screen: "Details for Allen Weisselberg"
Prosecutor: Does min mean minutes and does Verizon round up?
Tomalin: Yes.
Prosecutor: No further questions.

Justice Merchan: Cross?
Trump's lawyer Bove: The subscriber records are not redacted... Is Keith Davidson linked to this number?
Tomalin: Yes...
Bove: No further question.
Justice Merchan: We'll break. [Jurors leave]
Bove: We object to 1999 statements

Prosecutor: In the 1999 video [not yet in evidence] Mr. Trump speaks of campaign finance laws going back to 1907, it's relevant
Justice Merchan: I'll rule after the break.

[They're back...
Justice Merchan: 1999, it's too attenuate. Now you say you have only two more witnesses today? How long?
Prosecutor: A bit over an hour.
Justice Merchan: Shall we work to 1 pm or a bit past, and not come back in the afternoon?
Parties agree

Prosecutor: The People re-call Ms. Longstreet [DANY paralegal]
Justice Merchan: You are still under oath.
Prosecutor: Do you work with other paralegals on the Donald Trump case?
Longstreet: Yes.
[Trump at defense table is working on a piece of paper, with a pen

Prosecutor: Did you find and save public court filings that might be relevant to this prosecution?
Longstreet: Yes.
Prosecutor: How many relevant cases have you reviewed?
Longstreet: 75 cases.
Prosecutor: Is this a Twitter thread by at RealDonaldTrump?
A: Yes

[Thread asserts pressure's on Cohen to flip, then praises him.
Next tweet shown to jury: "If anyone is looking for a good lawyer, I would strongly suggest you do not retain Michael Cohen"]
Prosecutor: Is there an exclamation point at the end?
Longstreet: Yes!

Prosecutor [after showing a tweet praising Paul Manafort for, by contrast, not flipping] Is this a three-tweet thread?
Longstreet: Yes. May 3, 2018.
[Thread about NDA payment, "campaign

contributions played no part in this transaction"]

Prosecutor: Who redacted these text messages?
Longstreet: I did.
Prosecutor: Please read them?
Longstreet: This is from Gina Rodriguez to Dylan Howard: Stormy Daniels was his mistress... She will talk under two conditions

Prosecutor: Read these please, from July 31, 2016
Longstreet: Gina R to Dylan H: Whatever happened with the Stormy Daniels interview? Then on August 8, 2016, Call me
Prosecutor: And these?
Longstreet: Dylan H to Gina R: He likely will pay. How much? Gina R: 250K

Prosecutor: Please read this from October 8-9, 2016
Longstreet: "$120,000 - sold." Then Dylan H to Gina, I'm at dinner but will forward contract. Gina R to Dylan H, I haven't told

them anything accept [sic] what I said yesterday

Prosecutor: And this?
Longstreet: Gina H. to Dylan H. She's doing a press conference this morning, she hired another lawyer.
Prosecutor: No further questions.
Trump's lawyer Todd Blanche: I'm not going to re-ask you my questions from late Friday - 1000s of Tweets?

Trump's lawyer Blanche: You have not reviewed Michael Cohen's TikTok's for example from Wednesday night?
Longstreet: I have not.
Blanche: These texts you read, you have no personal knowledge if they are true or what they mean, do you?
Longstreet: I do not.

Blanche: No further questions.
Next witness is another DANY paralegal.
Paralegal: I reviewed call logs and related records: subscriber information in People's 401. We have a software that works with the

data AT&T provides. Verizon records were PDF, trickier

Prosecutor: Is People's 340 calls between Michael Cohen and David Pecker?
Paralegal: Yes.
Prosecutor: Is People's 349 calls between the Defendant and Michael Cohen?
Paralegal: Yes.
Prosecutor: Move to admit.
Trump's lawyer Blanche: No objection.
Admitted

Prosecutor: What are People's 1 through 34?
Paralegal: Checks and invoices.
Prosecutor: Move to admit this summary chart.
Trump's lawyer Bove: Objection to this, can we have a sidebar, please
[Sidebar]

[Trump continues flipping through and writing up papers during the sidebar. Then;]
Justice Merchan: We'll resolve your objection as discussed at the bench.
Prosecutor: When we are ready to display the

summary chart - People's 350

Bove: As modified, no objection

[Chart: 11 invoices, 12 vouchers, 11 checks [adds up to 34...]]

Prosecutor: Each lines up to a count of the indictment?

Paralegal: Yes.

Prosecutor: I have nothing further.

Trump's lawyer Bove: Was this tedious work?

Paralegal: Actually I kind of enjoyed it

Trump's lawyer Bove: From 2018, there are about a page and half of calls cut?

Paralegal: I don't know.

Bove: Look at the government's exhibit list of April 16, 2024. Look at 336 and 337 - some pages were deleted - was this after our cross of Davidson?

A: What?

Trump's lawyer Bove: And here, 344 - you deleted several pages?

Paralegal: Yes.

Bove: With Michael Cohen, remember CP1

and CP2? PX 247, that recording file off the physical device CP1, Sept 6, 2016. In PX 400, go to Bates 2726
Paralegal: Can I explain?
Bove: Qs

Trump's lawyer Bove: These are the IMEIs-
Paralegal: I think you're blowing up the wrong column
Bove: Now CP1 is using another IMEI - do you remember what Mr. Dixon said?
Paralegal: I don't want to contradict him
Bove: Nothing further

Re-direct
Prosecutor: Why did we shorting the charts?
Paralegal: To include only what came up at trial. We're pretty well down the road, s...
Prosecutor: Earlier you wanted to explain - what did you want to say?
Paralegal: Mr. Bovay, Bove, sorry, it was AT&T

Prosecutor: Do people sometimes get a new phone but keep the same phone number?
Paralegal: I do.

Prosecutor: Nothing further

Trump's lawyer Bove: You're just speculating, right?

Paralegal: The importance of the call is the time stamp.

Bove: The recording cuts off

Trump's lawyer Bove: Nothing further.

Justice Merchan: Jurors, you may leave. [They do] Mr. Blanche, any objection to me getting People's 350, to help me prepare the jury charge?

Blanche: We're fine with that. We intend to submit some proposed charges.

Prosecutor: We intend to call two witnesses and it is entirely possible we will rest by the end of the week.

Trump's lawyer Bove: The separation agreement between the Trump Organization & Allen Weisselberg, it's unduly prejudicial. And not relevant. He's in prison

Prosecutor: We want to explain why he is not here. There are three payments due to Mr. Weisselberg this year, $250,000 each. He

promised not to denigrate the company.
Trump's lawyer Bove: That's not why Mr. Weisselberg is not here. Mr. McConney has one too

Trump's lawyer Bove: The reason Mr. Weisselberg is not here is that the District Attorney decided to bring a perjury prosecution
Prosecutor: We'd stipulate that he's in prison for perjury
Justice Merchan: That could resolve it
Bove: no it wouldn't.

Justice Merchan: It would be helpful to me to see some effort to compel him to be here. It's a factor for me.
Prosecutor: We could subpoena him and put him up there cold.
Justice Merchan: We could do it out of the presence of the jury.

Trump's lawyer Bove: Mr. Weisselberg has never been on the government's witness list. We were barred today from introducing an exhibit -

Justice Merchan: It's different. You didn't think it was possible they would call Mr. Weisselberg?
Bove: Not from the list

Trump's lawyer Blanche: Mr. Cohen continues to go on TikTok, in a t-shirt with President Trump in jail on it - we ask you to order the People to order the witness to not talk about President Trump until the case is over.
Prosecutor: We tell me. We don't control it

Justice Merchan: I would direct the People to tell Mr. Cohen that the Judge is saying to not make any more public statements until the trial is over. Adjourned.

Chapter 16: [Jeff] McConney

Look I rarely talked to The Boss
But now they've got me
Running from court to court.

It wasn't my fault.
If Allen said Approve it
I did, to Deb Terasoff

Chapter 17: [Deb] Terasoff

When I came back to work
After my husband died
Trump Org seemed nice

I just cut the checks
Now all these subpoenas
And Mr. Trump looking at me. How?

And Michael Cohen? Next in a series, Inner City Press

www.ingramcontent.com/pod-product-compliance
Lightning Source LLC
Chambersburg PA
CBHW071211240526
45470CB00018B/1723